Stage 6
Floppy's Phonics
Kate Ruttle

Group/Guided 1

Contents

Introduction	2
Focus phonics	3
Vocabulary	4
Comprehension Strategies	5
Curriculum coverage charts	6

The Castle Garden
Group or guided reading	9
Group and independent reading activities	10
Speaking, listening and drama activities	11
Writing activities	12

Top Score
Group or guided reading	13
Group and independent reading activities	14
Speaking, listening and drama activities	15
Writing activities	16

Mum's Birthday Surprise
Group or guided reading	17
Group and independent reading activities	18
Speaking, listening and drama activities	19
Writing activities	20

A Rare Pair of Bears
Group or guided reading	21
Group and independent reading activities	22
Speaking, listening and drama activities	23
Writing activities	24

Change Gear! Steer!
Group or guided reading	25
Group and independent reading activities	26
Speaking, listening and drama activities	27
Writing activities	28

Uncle Max and the Treasure
Group or guided reading	29
Group and independent reading activities	30
Speaking, listening and drama activities	32
Writing activities	32

Introduction

Welcome to *Floppy's Phonics!* This series gives you decodable phonic stories featuring all your favourite *Oxford Reading Tree* characters. The books provide the perfect opportunity for consolidation and practice of synthetic phonics within a familiar setting, to build the children's confidence. As well as having a strong phonic focus, each story is a truly satisfying read with lots of opportunities for comprehension, so they are fully in line with the simple view of reading.

Phonic development

The *Floppy's Phonics* stories support a synthetic phonics approach to early reading skills. They should be used for practice and consolidation. The books should be read in the suggested order (see chart on page 3), so that children can benefit from the controlled introduction, revision and consolidation of the phonemes. They can be used alongside core Oxford Reading Tree *Songbirds*, which introduces the same phonemes in the same order. In addition, they can be used for practice and consolidation after introducing the sounds with other programmes.

Stage 6 of the series can be used within Phase 5 of *Letters and Sounds*, to support children as they broaden their knowledge of graphemes and phonemes for use in reading and spelling. The books will help to embed these vital early phonics skills, and help to ensure that children will experience success in reading and thus will be motivated to keep on reading.

The children will benefit most from reading *Floppy's Phonics Stage 6* if they are:

- able to recognize that phonemes can be represented in different ways, and that many graphemes can also be pronounced in different ways
- able to blend and segment words including long vowel phonemes.

Focus phonics

This chart shows which phonemes are introduced and practised in each title.

Title	ORT Stage Book band colour Year group	Focus phonics	Phonic concept to be introduced	Focus phonics revisited
The Castle Garden	Stage 6 Orange Year 2	/ar/ as in *garden* (made by *ar, a*)	The same phoneme can be represented in a number of ways (all books)	/ee/ as in *need* /oo/ as in *choose*
Top Score	Stage 6 Orange Year 2	/au/ as in *score* (made by *or, au, aw, oor, a, ar*)		/ai/ as in *Craig*
Mum's Birthday Surprise	Stage 6 Orange Year 2	/ur/ as in *birthday* (made by *er, ir, ur, ear, or*)		/ee/ as in *need* /oo/ as in *could* /ai/ as in *stay*
A Rare Pair of Bears	Stage 6 Orange Year 2	/air/ as in *fair* (made by *air, are, ear, ere, a*)		/ow/ as in *pounds* /ur/ as in *worth*
Change Gear! Steer!	Stage 6 Orange Year 2	/ear/ as in *gear* (made by *ear, ier, eer, ere, ea*)		/s/ as in *race* /ee/ as in *screen* /au/ as in *warning* /ow/ as in *crowd*
Uncle Max and the Treasure	Stage 6 Orange Year 2	/ure/ as in *sure* (made by *ure, ur*); /j/ as in *gems* (made by *dge, g, j, ge*)	A letter pattern can represent more than one sound (same grapheme, different phoneme)	/ar/ as in *hard* /au/ as in *story* /ur/ as in *Turkey* /air/ as in *there* /eer/ as in *steer*

Vocabulary

The Castle Garden	Decodable words	part start far large garden smart grassy Charley Tara partner darling cards charming Jimjar hard parking carts carpets yards hand-crafted jars park pardon Carl gardener asked castle paths Father Shah France chance after ah can't Master
	Tricky words	Anneena lived perfume voice always happily princess prince expensive Tarquin Kazar Candibar Tsar ghastly
Top Score	Decodable words	scorpion sport for force morning Corex Norman Thorkel horns horned horses Norse Thor story recorded more score wore Augan Gaul crawly claws claw awful draw drawings straw Hawk saw door floor poor all call hall wall talk war fallen brought fought thought
	Tricky words	awesome applause naughty swords enormous Nadim school Viking Vikings axes plastic right
Mum's Birthday Surprise	Decodable words	her perfume Fern person certainly pearls pearl girl birthday thirty thirteen firm turn Thursday surprise purse burst purple turtle heard earn learns earth mermaid word firework(s) world worst worth
	Tricky words	performed purchase favourite expensive whoosh crazy icing diving amazed concert loved wanted pulled
A Rare Pair of Bears	Decodable words	chair airship fair fairly fairy hair pair repair unfair upstairs Mary stared bare beware care careful dare nightmare rare scare share spare bear tear wear bears where there thousands pounds round found
	Tricky words	another many periscope woman gasped stolen quicker called money
Change Gear! Steer!	Decodable words	nearly year clear fear rear gear clearing dear pier cheer steer veered steering sheer cheered here really every his dad went seaside like it to go the with was on they have games in said wow car
	Tricky words	severe arcade select driver exciting Racing Ace forest liked called yelled slowed spoiler warning corner mountain wrong
Uncle Max and the Treasure	Decodable words	you're sure fury pure Ginger Jones gems jewels gone Fingers ridge edge ages story story-teller before bore fall snore floor pour four shore storm for called saw tall all Martha are hard ah curled turkey turned were first work there chair beware fair share spare scarce careful years steer sheer here
	Tricky words	measure luxury treasure curious furious picture secure adventure oh yelled couldn't didn't rowed smashed island wind fire pirate secret love

Decodable words

Most of the common words introduced in *Floppy's Phonics* are phonically decodable, using phonics skills and knowledge that has been gradually developed through *Floppy's Phonics*. Certain words may have been tricky to read initially (e.g. *could, said*) but should be easily recognizable by this phase.

Tricky words

Tricky words are words which contain unusual grapheme-phoneme correspondences (e.g. *was, every*). The advice in *Letters and Sounds* is that children should be taught to recognize the phonemes they know within these words and to distinguish these from the tricky bits. For example, in the word *called*, children should be taught to recognize the grapheme *all* and then to recognise it in words like *call, talk*. Certain tricky words in *Floppy's Phonics* have been used because of the particular context of a story. They may be phonically advanced or phonically irregular (e.g. *Kipper, treasure*). These have been kept to a minimum and should be easily predicted by children.

Comprehension Strategies

Reading is about making meaning, and it is particularly important that a child's earliest reading books offer opportunities for making meaning and telling a complete story. As with all *Oxford Reading Tree* stories, the titles in *Floppy's Phonics* are fun stories which children will really enjoy, and which will give you lots of scope for practising and extending their comprehension skills.

Story	Comprehension strategy taught through these Teaching Notes				
	Prediction	Questioning	Clarifying	Summarizing	Imagining
The Castle Garden	✓	✓		✓	✓
Top Score	✓	✓		✓	
Mum's Birthday Surprise	✓		✓		✓
A Rare Pair of Bears	✓	✓		✓	
Change Gear! Steer!	✓	✓	✓	✓	
Uncle Max and the Treasure	✓	✓			✓

Curriculum coverage chart

	Speaking, listening, drama	Reading	Writing
The Castle Garden			
PNS Literacy Framework (Y2)	1.2	Ⓦ 5.1, 5.3, 5.4	10.1
National Curriculum	Working towards level 2		
Scotland (5–14) (P3)	Level B	Level B	Level B
N. Ireland (P3/Y3)	1, 2, 3, 4, 5, 6	1, 2, 3, 4, 8, 11, 12, 14, 15, 16, 17	1, 2, 3, 5, 8
Wales Key Stage 1	Range: 1, 5 Skills: 1, 2, 3, 4, 5	Range: 1, 2, 4, 5, 6 Skills: 1, 2	Range: 2, 3, 5 Skills: 6, 7, 8
Top Score			
PNS Literacy Framework (Y2)	3.3	Ⓦ 5.3, 5.4, 6.1	9.3
National Curriculum	Working towards level 2		
Scotland (5–14) (P3)	Level B	Level B	Level B
N. Ireland (P3/Y3)	1, 2, 3, 6, 9	1, 2, 3, 4, 8, 11, 12, 14, 15, 16, 17	1, 4, 6, 7, 8, 10
Wales Key Stage 1	Range: 1, 3, 5 Skills: 1, 2, 3, 4, 5, 6	Range: 1, 2, 4, 5, 6 Skills: 1, 2	Range: 1, 2, 3, 4, 5 Skills: 5, 6, 7, 8

Key

Ⓒ = Language comprehension   Y = Year

Ⓦ = Word recognition   P = Primary

In the designations such as 5.2, the first number represents the strand and the second number the individual objective

Curriculum coverage chart

	Speaking, listening, drama	Reading	Writing
Mum's Birthday Surprise			
PNS Literacy Framework (Y2)	4.2	Ⓦ 5.3, 5.4, 6.1	9.4
National Curriculum	Working towards level 2		
Scotland (5–14) (P3)	Level B	Level B	Level B
N. Ireland (P3/Y3)	1, 2, 3, 6, 7, 11	1, 2, 3, 4, 5, 8, 11, 12, 14, 15, 16, 17	1, 2, 3, 4, 7, 8, 10
Wales Key Stage 1	Range: 1, 3, 5, 6 Skills: 1, 2, 3, 5	Range: 1, 2, 4, 5, 6 Skills: 1, 2	Range: 1, 3, 5, 7 Skills: 1, 5, 7, 8
A Rare Pair of Bears			
PNS Literacy Framework (Y2)	3.3	Ⓦ 5.1, 5.3, 5.4	10.1
National Curriculum	Working towards level 2		
Scotland (5–14) (P3)	Level B	Level B	Level B
N. Ireland (P3/Y3)	1, 2, 5, 6, 7, 8, 10, 12	1, 2, 3, 4, 5, 8, 11, 12, 14, 15, 16, 17	1, 3, 4, 8, 10
Wales Key Stage 1	Range: 1, 3, 5 Skills: 1, 2, 3, 4, 5	Range: 1, 2, 4, 5, 6 Skills: 1, 2	Range: 2, 3, 4, 5 Skills: 5, 6, 7, 8

Curriculum coverage chart

	Speaking, listening, drama	Reading	Writing
Change Gear! Steer!			
PNS Literacy Framework (Y2)	7.1	(W) 5.2, 5.4, 5.5	11.1
National Curriculum	Working towards level 2		
Scotland (5–14) (P3)	Level B	Level B	Level B
N. Ireland (P3/Y3)	1, 2, 3, 5, 6, 7, 9	1, 2, 3, 4, 5, 8, 11, 12, 14, 15, 16, 17	1, 2, 3, 4, 6, 8
Wales Key Stage 1	Range: 3 Skills: 2, 3, 4, 5	Range: 1, 2, 4, 5, 6 Skills: 1, 2	Range: 1, 3, 4, 5, 7 Skills: 1, 5, 6, 7, 8
Uncle Max and the Treasure			
PNS Literacy Framework (Y2)	1.2	(W) 5.3, 5.4, 6.1	9.2
National Curriculum	Working towards level 2		
Scotland (5–14) (P3)	Level B	Level B	Level B
N. Ireland (P3/Y3)	1, 2, 3, 4, 6, 7, 9, 10, 11	1, 2, 3, 4, 5, 8, 11, 12, 14, 15, 16, 17	1, 2, 3, 4, 6, 8, 10
Wales Key Stage 1	Range: 1, 2, 5 Skills: 1, 2, 3, 4, 5	Range: 1, 2, 4, 5, 6 Skills: 1, 2	Range: 1, 2, 3, 5, 7 Skills: 1, 3, 4, 5, 6, 7, 8

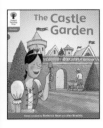

The Castle Garden

> **C** = Language comprehension   **R, AF** = QCA reading assessment focus
> **W** = Word recognition   **W, AF** = QCA writing assessment focus

Focus phonics:

Focus phonics in this book: /ar/ as in 'garden' (made by ar, a (Southern accents only))

Phonemes revisited include: /ee/ as in 'need' (made by ee, ea, y, e); /oo/ as in 'choose' (made by oo, u-e, ou)

Group or guided reading

Introducing the book

W Can the children read the title? Remind them of the silent *t* in *castle*. Which words can they hear with the long vowel phoneme /ar/? Read the title: *Th-e C-a-s-t-le G-ar-d-e-n*.

C *(Prediction)* Encourage children to use prediction. Look at the cover picture and the blurb. What can they tell you about the story? Can they predict what might happen in the castle garden?

W Turn to page 1. Remind the children to use their phonic knowledge to read the text. Which letter patterns representing the long vowel phoneme /ar/ can they identify? (*ar*)

• Look through the book, talking about what happens on each page. Use some of the high frequency words as you discuss the story.

Strategy check

Remind the children to sound out words carefully, remembering that two letters can represent one sound, particularly one vowel sound, and also that the same letter can often be pronounced in more than one way. If the children can't sound out a word, what other strategies can they use?

Independent reading

- Sample the children's reading as they read the story aloud. Praise and encourage them while they read, and prompt as necessary.
- **(C)** *(Prediction)* Ask the children what they think might happen after the end of the story.

Assessment Check that children:

- *(R, AF1)* use phonic knowledge to sound out and blend the phonemes in words (see chart on page 3)
- *(R, AF2)* use comprehension skills to work out what is happening
- *(R, AF1)* make a note of any difficulties the children encounter and of strategies they use to solve problems.

Returning to the text

(C) *(Questioning)* Ask: *Do you think Tara loved Carl before he said that he loved her?*

Assessment *(R, AF3)* Can the children evaluate possible answers to the question and decide on their own?

Group and independent reading activities

Objective Read and spell less common graphemes (5.4).

- **(W)** Ask all the children in the group to read the following words: *cat, cart, castle, class.* The children should listen hard as each child speaks, and then decide how many different ways there are of pronouncing the vowel phoneme /ar/.
- In different regional accents, this set of words will be pronounced differently. You will need to be sensitive to the children's accents as you teach the phoneme /ar/.
- Give each child a set of the words. Ask them to find other words with the same spelling and pronunciation in the book.

Assessment *(R, AF1)* Can the children read the words *grass, gather* and *garden* and tell you which words are pronounced with the same vowel phoneme?

Objective Know how to tackle unfamiliar words that are not completely decodable (5.3).

- (W) Look again at the book's title. Can the children identify the 'tricky bit' in the word *castle*? What do they remember about silent letters?
- Challenge the children to find more silent letters on pages 16–18 (silent letters in *Tsar, knight, ghastly*).
- Discuss why the *gh* in *knight* and the *r* in *garden* are not silent letters. (They are part of the letter pattern that represents the long vowel each time.)
- Talk about strategies for reading when you can't simply sound out the word letter by letter.

Assessment *(R, AF1)* Can children suggest other words with silent letters in them?

Objective Read independently and with increasing fluency (5.1).

- (W) **You will need:** either a PC and a USB microphone or an audio-cassette recorder and microphone.
- Tape each of the children while they read two pages aloud from the book. At the beginning of the tape, read two pages yourself as a model of fluent reading.
- Listen together to all of the readings. Ask each child to comment on what they need to do to become more fluent readers. Help them to identify useful strategies and skills. Let each child set their own target for reading fluently.

Assessment *(R, AF1)* Can each child set a reasonable target? Give them a few weeks to work towards it and then revisit the target in the same way with a different book.

Speaking, listening and drama activities

Objective Tell imagined stories using the conventions of familiar story language (1.2).

- (C) *(Imagining)* Reread the story, talking about what is happening at each stage.
- Ask the children to draw four pictures, each one representing an important event in the story.

- Ask the children to work in pairs to think of answers to Biff's question at the end of the story. They then practise retelling the whole story, including their ending, using their pictures.
- Children then swap partners to tell their stories.

Assessment *(R, AF5)* Can children use conventions of story language when retelling their stories?

Writing activities

Objective Use planning to establish clear sections for writing (10.1).

- **C** *(Summarizing)* Ask the children to add at least two more pictures to their story summary.
- As the children then write their stories, remind them to use the pictures for sections in their writing.

Assessment *(W, AF4)* Can children write in sections based on their pictures?

Top Score

C = Language comprehension   **R, AF** = QCA reading assessment focus
W = Word recognition   **W, AF** = QCA writing assessment focus

Focus phonics:

Focus phonics in this book: /au/ as in 'score' (made by or, au, aw, oor, a, ar)

Phonemes revisited include: /ai/ as in 'Craig' (made by ai, a-e, ay)

Group or guided reading

Introducing the book

W Can the children read the title? Which words can they hear with the phoneme /au/? Read the title: *T-o-p S-c-or-e*.

C *(Prediction)* Encourage the children to use prediction. Look at the cover picture and the blurb. What can they tell you about the story? Ask: *What might 'Top Score' refer to?*

W Turn to page 1. Remind children to use their phonic knowledge to read the text. Which letter patterns representing the long vowel phoneme /au/ can they identify? (*au, ough, or, aw*)

- Look through the book, talking about what happens on each page. Use some of the high frequency words as you discuss the story.

Strategy check

Remind the children to sound out words carefully, remembering that two letters can represent one sound, particularly one vowel sound, and also that the same letter can often be pronounced in more than one way. If children can't sound out a word, what other strategies can they use?

Independent reading

- Sample the children's reading as they read the story aloud. Praise and encourage them while they read, and prompt as necessary.

C *(Questioning)* Ask: *Do you think Mrs May is a good sport? Why/Why not?*

Assessment Check that children:

- *(R, AF1)* use phonic knowledge to sound out and blend the phonemes in words (see chart on page 3)
- *(R, AF2)* use comprehension skills to work out what is happening
- *(R, AF1)* make a note of any difficulties the children encounter and of strategies they use to solve problems.

Returning to the text

C *(Questioning)* Ask: *What was the most interesting thing the boys found out about the Vikings?*

Assessment *(R, AF3)* Can the children evaluate possible answers to the question and decide on their own?

Group and independent reading activities

Objective Read and spell less common graphemes including trigraphs (5.4).

W Prepare individual cards, each with one of the graphemes: *or, oor, au, aw, a, ar*.

- Clarify that all of these graphemes *can* represent the phoneme /au/. Discuss the graphemes. Ask: *Which are the most easily recognizable? Which are the trickiest?*
- Shuffle and randomly distribute the cards amongst the children. Ask each of the children to quickly find a word containing each of their graphemes.
- Ask: *Which of the graphemes was easiest to find in a word? Why? (Is it the most common?) Which was hardest? Why?*

Assessment *(R, AF1)* Can each child read the words that a different child found?

Objective Spell, drawing on knowledge of word structure, including common inflections (6.1).

- **(W)** Look at page 1 and ask children to identify the suffixes – word endings that are added to a base word (*ing, y, ly*). Can the children tell you what each word would be, with and without these endings?
- Give individuals or pairs of children different pages to look at, each time with the aim of finding word endings. Ask the children to jot down the whole word each time and underline the suffix.
- Talk about the suffixes the children found. Ask: *Which were the most common? Which were hard to spot?*

Assessment *(W, AF8)* Can children recognize common suffixes in their reading and spelling?

Objective Know how to tackle unfamiliar words that are not completely decodable (5.3).

- **(W)** Ask each child to revisit the book and find three words that they think other groups of children might get stuck on.
- Ask the children to suggest ways of reading the words that might help the other children.
- Identify any other words that this group found difficulty with and discuss strategies for decoding the words.

Assessment *(R, AF1)* Can the children both identify tricky words and suggest strategies for reading them?

Speaking, listening and drama activities

Objective Listen to each other's views and preferences (3.3).

- **(C)** *(Summarizing)* Reread the story, focusing particularly on the work the boys did in finding out about the Vikings.
- Talk together about how the boys worked on their presentation. Use evidence from the text.
- Ask each child in your group to explain one fact about the Vikings that the boys found out. Can the second child repeat that fact, and then add another? The third child should repeat the first two facts and add their own, and so on.

- Ask each child to explain which they thought was the most interesting of the Viking facts and why.

Assessment *(R, AF5)* Can the children listen to each other successfully?

Writing activities

Objective Maintain consistency in non-narrative, including purpose and tense (9.3).

C *(Summarizing)* Ask the children to write or type a short text on the Vikings using facts from this story.

Assessment *(W, AF3)* Can the children select only facts and present them in an appropriate, non-narrative style?

Mum's Birthday Surprise

> **C** = Language comprehension **R, AF** = QCA reading assessment focus
> **W** = Word recognition **W, AF** = QCA writing assessment focus

Focus phonics:

Focus phonics in this book: /ur/ as in 'birthday' (made by er, ir, ur, ear, or)

Phonemes revisited include: /ee/ as in 'need' (made by ee, ea, y); /oo/ as in 'could'; /ai/ as in 'stay' (made by ay, ai, a-e)

Group or guided reading

Introducing the book

W Can the children read the title? Help the children identify the words with the phoneme /ur/ (B<u>ir</u>thday S<u>ur</u>prise). Read the title: *Mum's B-ir-th-d-ay S-ur-p-r-i-s-e.*

C *(Prediction)* Encourage the children to use prediction by looking at the cover picture and the blurb. Can they predict what Mum's surprise might be?

W Turn to page 1. Remind the children to use their phonic knowledge to read the text. Which letter patterns representing the long vowel phoneme /ur/ can they identify? (*ir, ur, er*)

- Look through the book, talking about what happens on each page. Use some of the high frequency words as you discuss the story.

Strategy check

Remind the children to sound out words carefully, remembering that two letters can represent one sound, particularly one vowel sound, and also that the same letters can often be pronounced in more than one way. If children can't sound out a word, what other strategies can they use?

Independent reading

- Sample the children's reading as they read the story aloud. Praise and encourage them while they read, and prompt as necessary.

C *(Questioning)* Ask the children what they think of Uncle Max's story. Is it true?

Assessment Check that children:

- *(R, AF1)* use phonic knowledge to sound out and blend the phonemes in words (see chart on page 3)
- *(R, AF2)* use comprehension skills to work out what is happening
- *(R, AF1)* make a note of any difficulties the children encounter and of strategies they use to solve problems.

Returning to the text

C *(Clarifying)* Ask: *What was Mum's birthday surprise?*

Assessment *(R, AF3)* Can the children explain what Mum's birthday surprise was?

Group and independent reading activities

Objective Read and spell less common graphemes including trigraphs (5.4).

W Play *Phoneme spotter*. Read the text aloud. The children put their hands up when they hear a word with /ur/ or they can keep a tally if they know how to.

- Agree how many /ur/ words there are in total in the book (not including the title). There are at least 29.
- Now ask the children to work in pairs to do a 'word sort'. They organize the words into sets of words where the /ur/ phoneme is spelled the same way.
- Discuss which spelling is the most common in this book.

Assessment *(R, AF1)* Can the children identify and sort the /ur/ words correctly?

Objective Know how to tackle unfamiliar words that are not completely decodable (5.3).

W Make a list of the longer 'tricky' words in the book, for example: *expensive, seventeen, certainly, amazed, favourite, concert, performed.*

- Discuss how to tackle each of the words: which are compound words, which have suffixes etc.
- Identify the 'tricky bit' in the words.
- Explicitly agree strategies for tackling harder-looking words.

Assessment *(R, AF1)* Can the children explain which strategies they use when they read a tricky word?

Objective Spell with increasing accuracy and confidence (6.1).

- **(W)** Ask each child to choose six words with the /ur/ phoneme from the book and give those words to a partner.
- Each child should look at their words and consider strategies for remembering how to spell them – and which way they have to represent /ur/ in each word.
- Ask each child to give their partner a quiz to see how well they have learned the words.
- Share strategies across the group.

Assessment *(R, AF1)* Can the children explain their strategies for remembering the words? Do the strategies work effectively?

Speaking, listening and drama activities

Objective Present part of a story for members of their own class (4.2).

- **(C)** *(Imagining)* Reread the story, focusing particularly on Uncle Max's story.
- Ask the children to work together in small groups to perform his story, just like the children did in the book.
- Let the children perform the story to other groups, or to the whole class.
- Ask all the children to critique their own performances.

Assessment *(R, AF5)* Can the children make good assessments of their performances?

Writing activities

Objective Make adventurous word and language choices appropriate to the style and purpose of the text (9.4).

C *(Imagining)* Look again at the story and pictures of Uncle Max finding the pearl.

- The language Uncle Max uses is very simple. Explore some descriptive phrases to talk about the sea, the underwater creatures, the mermaid and the pearl.
- Ask the children to retell Uncle Max's story, but using more descriptive language so that people without the pictures in front of them can imagine the scene in their heads.

Assessment *(W, AF1)* Can the children write an interesting, descriptive story based on Uncle Max's original tale?

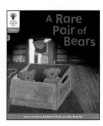

A Rare Pair of Bears

> **C** = Language comprehension **R, AF** = QCA reading assessment focus
> **W** = Word recognition **W, AF** = QCA writing assessment focus

Focus phonics:

Focus phonics in this book: /air/ as in 'fair' (made by air, are, ear, ere, a)

Phonemes revisited include: /ow/ as in 'pounds' (made by ow, ou); /ur/ as in 'worth' (made by ir, or, er)

Group or guided reading

Introducing the book

(W) Can the children read the title? Which words can they hear with the phoneme /air/? (R*are*, P*air*, B*ears*) Read the title: *A R-are P-air o-f B-ear-s*.

(C) *(Prediction)* Encourage the children to use prediction by looking at the cover picture and the blurb. Ask: *Why might the bears be rare?*

(W) Turn to pages 1–3. Remind the children to use their phonic knowledge to read the text. Which letter patterns representing the long vowel phoneme /air/ can they identify? (*air, are, ear, ere*) Point out that the *a* in *Mary* is a very uncommon representation of /air/ (also in *vary* and *wary*).

- Look through the book, talking about what happens on each page. Use some of the high frequency words as you discuss the story.

Strategy check

Remind the children to sound out words carefully, remembering that two letters can represent one sound, particularly one vowel sound, and also that the same letters can often be pronounced in more than one way. If children can't sound out a word, what other strategies can they use?

Independent reading

- Sample the children's reading as they read the story aloud. Praise and encourage them while they read, and prompt as necessary.

(C) *(Questioning)* Ask: *Why might the woman in the red coat want to steal Gran's bears?*

Assessment Check that children:

- *(R, AF1)* use phonic knowledge to sound out and blend the phonemes in words (see chart on page 3)
- *(R, AF2)* use comprehension skills to work out what is happening
- *(R, AF1)* make a note of any difficulties the children encounter and of strategies they use to solve problems.

Returning to the text

(C) *(Questioning)* Ask: *Was it good that Gran sold the bears?*

Assessment *(R, AF3)* Can the children evaluate possible answers to the question and decide on their own?

Group and independent reading activities

Objective Read and spell less common graphemes including trigraphs (5.4).

(W) You will need: cards showing the words: *rare, spare, share, scare; pair, chair, stair, repair; bear, wear, tear, pear;* as well as cards with the graphemes: *air, ear, are.*

- Put the children into teams, and give each team a grapheme card.
- Shuffle the cards in your hands, so the children can't see them. Look at the top word and say it, together with a sentence to clarify homophones.
- Look for the first child to put up their hand and claim the word for their team. If they are right, give them the word and one point. If they are wrong, deduct a point.

Assessment *(R, AF1)* Can the children think about the spelling when they hear the word?

Objective Know how to tackle unfamiliar words that are not completely decodable (5.3).

(W) Ask the children to look through the book and jot down all words with *o*, either on its own or as part of a spelling pattern (for example *or, ough*). Give children different pages to search through.

- Let the children do a 'word sort' of all the words, writing them according to how the *o* is pronounced on a big sheet of paper.
- Discuss the 'oddities' like *money, woman, over, worth.* Talk about strategies for reading and pronouncing the words in context.

Assessment *(R, AF1)* Can the children explain which strategies they use when they read a tricky word?

Objective Read independently and with increasing fluency (5.1).

(W) Model reading the first three pages of the book and ask the children for feedback on your reading. Are they aware of the way you:
- read with no hesitation between words;
- use expression to make your reading aloud interesting;
- make your voice reflect the punctuation by pausing at full stops or putting an emphasis on the first word in the speech marks?

- Ask the children to choose a double page spread from the book and to practise reading it aloud.
- Let the children read to response partners. The child who read should first say what they thought they did successfully and what they need to improve; then the response partner should do the same.

Assessment *(R, AF1)* Can the children self-assess their reading accurately and give useful feedback?

Speaking, listening and drama activities

Objective Listen to each other's views and preferences (3.3).

(C) *(Questioning)* Do a hot-seating drama activity with Gran in the hot seat.
- Ask children to reread the book, thinking of questions to ask Gran. You could help them with some of the questions to begin with.
- During the question and answer session, encourage discussion rather than simply answering the questions.

Assessment *(R, AF5)* Can the children think of questions and then listen politely to each others' views?

Writing activities

Objective Use planning to establish clear sections for writing (10.1).

- **C** *(Summarizing)* Ask the children to write a character report on Gran, based on the events in the book.
- They should begin by mind-mapping to establish the headings for their report.

Assessment *(W, AF3)* Can the children summarize their understanding of Gran in a well-planned report?

Change Gear! Steer!

> **C** = Language comprehension   **R, AF** = QCA reading assessment focus
> **W** = Word recognition   **W, AF** = QCA writing assessment focus

Focus phonics:

Focus phonics in this book: /ear/ as in 'gear' (made by ear, ier, eer, ere, ea)

Phonemes revisited include: /s/ as in 'race' (made by ce, s); /ee/ as in 'screen' (made by ea, ee, y); /au/ as in 'warning' (made by ar, or); /ow/ as in 'crowd' (made by ow, ou)

Group or guided reading

Introducing the book

- **W** Can the children read the title? Which words can they hear with the phoneme /ear/? (G*ear*, St*eer*) Read the title: *Ch-a-n-ge G-ear! S-t-eer!*

- **C** *(Prediction)* Encourage the children to use prediction. Look at the cover picture and the blurb. Ask: *What is Nadim doing?*

- **W** Turn to pages 1–3. Remind the children to use their phonic knowledge to read the text. Which letter patterns representing the long vowel phoneme /ear/ can they identify? (Depending on the accent, look out for: *ear, ere, ier.*) Point out that the *ier* in *pier* is a very uncommon representation of /ear/.

- Look through the book, talking about what happens on each page. Use some of the high frequency words as you discuss the story.

Strategy check

Remind the children to sound out words carefully, remembering that two letters can represent one sound, particularly one vowel sound, and also that the same letters can often be pronounced in more than one way. If children can't sound out a word, what other strategies can they use?

Independent reading

- Sample the children's reading as they read the story aloud. Praise and encourage them while they read, and prompt as necessary.

Change Gear! Steer!

C *(Questioning)* Ask: *Who drove with the greatest skill?*

Assessment Check that children:

- *(R, AF1)* use phonic knowledge to sound out and blend the phonemes in words (see chart on page 3)
- *(R, AF2)* use comprehension skills to work out what is happening
- *(R, AF1)* make a note of any difficulties the children encounter and of strategies they use to solve problems.

Returning to the text

C *(Clarifying)* Ask: *Why did people gather in a crowd to watch Nadim and his dad?*

Assessment *(R, AF3)* Can the children explain why people may have wanted to watch Nadim and his dad on the racing game?

Group and independent reading activities

Objective Spell with increasing accuracy, drawing on knowledge of word structure and spelling patterns (5.2).

W **You will need:** cards showing the words: *near, real, clear, rear, cheer, steer, gear, veer, severe, sheer* as well as suffixes: *s, ly, ing, ed.*

- Ask the children to read all of the words. Discuss any difficulties and clarify which graphemes represent the phoneme /ear/.
- Make lists of all the words that each of the suffixes can be added to. Talk about how the new words can be used (none of the suffixes change the basic meaning of the word, they change single words to plural words, verbs to adverbs, parts of the verb, the verb tense, etc.).
- Show the children the base forms of each word and ask them to write the words with suffixes added. Does the spelling have to change when the suffixes are added?

Assessment *(W, AF8)* Can the children spell the words with the suffix added?

Objective Read high and medium frequency words independently and automatically (5.5).

W Let the children read the book aloud to a response partner. Each child in the pair should read a double page spread, then let their partner read the next. You can sample listening to the pairs at work.

- When children are listening, they should note down all of the words their partner hesitates over, sounds out, omits or gets wrong.
- Let pairs of children discuss the words they have noted down. What kinds of words are the children hesitating over?
- Talk in a group about words that are often not read automatically. Can children discuss strategies for recognizing the words next time?

Assessment *(R, AF1)* Can the children read most of the high frequency words in the text without hesitation?

Objective Read and spell less common alternative graphemes (5.4).

W In pairs, ask the children to collect /ear/ words from the book.
- Each child in each pair should choose five words to learn to spell.
- Let the children make pairs games, each child writing their five different words out twice. The children can mix up the words and play the game.
- Ask the children to test each other on their chosen words.

Assessment *(W, AF8)* Does the children's spelling of /ear/ words improve in their writing?

Speaking, listening and drama activities

Objective Draw together ideas from across a whole text (7.1).

C *(Summarizing)* Let the children work together to find all the information in the book about the route that Nadim and his dad steered.
- Using information and pictures from the book, children work together to construct a plan of the whole route.

Assessment *(R, AF3)* Can the children combine knowledge and information from across the whole book?

Writing activities

Objective Write simple and compound sentences (11.1).

C *(Summarizing)* Ask the children to use their plan of the route to write a guide on how to drive the route quickly and safely. Remind them that they should write both what the features are and how to drive around them safely.

- Encourage children to use words like: *first, then, after, because, so*.

Assessment *(W, AF6)* Can the children write well-constructed and informative sentences, indicating the relationship of events?

Uncle Max and the Treasure

> **C** = Language comprehension **R, AF** = QCA reading assessment focus
> **W** = Word recognition **W, AF** = QCA writing assessment focus

Focus phonics:

Focus phonics in this book: /ure/ as in 'sure' (made by ure, ur); /j/ as in 'gems' (made by dge, g, j, ge)

Phonemes revisited include: /ar/, /au/, /ur/, /air/, /ear/

Group or guided reading

Introducing the book

W Can the children read the title? Can they say how many phonemes there are in *Treasure*? (5) Read the title: *U-n-c-le M-a-x a-n-d th-e T-r-ea-s-ure*.

C *(Prediction)* Encourage the children to use prediction. Look at the cover picture and the blurb. Ask: *Where will Uncle Max find his treasure?*

W Turn to pages 2–3. How many words can the children find that rhyme with *snore?* Is *sure* one of them? Talk about the vowel phoneme in *sure*.

- Look through the book, talking about what happens on each page. Use some of the high frequency words as you discuss the story.

Strategy check

Remind the children to sound out words carefully, remembering that two letters can represent one sound, particularly one vowel sound, and also that the same letters can often be pronounced in more than one way. If children can't sound out a word, what other strategies can they use?

Independent reading

- Sample the children's reading as they read the story aloud. Praise and encourage them while they read, and prompt as necessary.

C *(Questioning)* Ask: *What did Uncle Max find when he returned to the island?*

Assessment Check that children:
- *(R, AF1)* use phonic knowledge to sound out and blend the phonemes in words (see chart on page 3)
- *(R, AF2)* use comprehension skills to work out what is happening
- *(R, AF1)* make a note of any difficulties the children encounter and of strategies they use to solve problems.

Returning to the text

C *(Questioning)* Ask: *How did Uncle Max feel about Fingers Foster at the end of the story?*

Assessment *(R, AF3)* Can children evaluate possible answers to the question and decide on their own?

Group and independent reading activities

Objective Read and spell less common graphemes (5.4).

W Give different pairs of children a few pages of the book to study.
- Ask the children to read their pages and to note all the phonemes which occur more than three times – include both consonant and vowel phonemes. They should then list all of the words which include those phonemes.
- Share the lists together. Ask: *Which phonemes occur most often in this book? Which are the most common spelling patterns used to represent those phonemes?*
- Compare the words different children have in their lists. Does everyone in the group pronounce all of the words in the same way? Focus on vowels found in words such as *sure*. Do children rhyme *sure* and *poor*? Do any children pronounce a different vowel? Are there any other vowels which children with different accents pronounce differently?

Assessment *(R, AF1)* Can children identify vowel phonemes and recognize their associated spelling patterns?

Objective Know how to tackle unfamiliar words that are not completely decodable (5.3).

- **(W)** Write a selection of potentially tricky words from the book, for example: *treasure, measure, adventure, curious, secure, luxury; island; pirate; secret.*
- Discuss with the children what they need to know in order to read the words successfully. This could include:
  - understanding of syllables;
  - understanding that a letter pattern can be pronounced in more than one way;
  - recognizing silent letters.
- Are there any other barriers to reading these words?
- Discuss whether these words are easier to read in the book or in isolation. Discuss the value of using the context when the words are not entirely decodable.

Assessment *(R, AF1)* Can the children use the named strategies to try to read these words?

Objective Spell with increasing accuracy and confidence (6.1).

- **(W)** Choose some words with more than one syllable, for example: *adventure, treasure, story, fury, letter, turkey, island, ages, luxury.*
- Ask the children to write three of the words on slips of paper and then cut each word up into its syllables. Check that the children are confident about where the syllable boundaries fall. They should know that syllables always have a vowel phoneme and often have consonants around the vowel.
- The children should then examine each syllable in their words to identify the 'tricky bit'. Let them talk to a partner to agree a way of remembering how to spell that tricky bit.
- Let the children test each other and see if they can remember how to spell their words.

Assessment *(W, AF8)* Can the children spell the words having studied them in this way?

Speaking, listening and drama activities

Objective Tell imagined stories using the conventions of familiar story language (1.2).

C *(Imagining)* Let the children work in pairs to explore their own version of this story. The story should include pirates, treasure and a map. Once children have worked out what happens in their story, they should prepare to tell the story to the group.

Assessment *(R, AF3)* Can the children tell a story, based on that in the book, using conventions of story language?

Writing activities

Objective Sustain form in narrative, including use of person and time (9.2).

C *(Imagining)* Ask the children to plan and write the story they told.
- Remind them about the use of story language from the book.

Assessment *(W, AF1)* Can the children write an interesting story, based on that in the book?